HOUSE OF LORDS INFORM.

Publications Series No

GW01032859

THE
LORD CHANCELLOR

Maurice Bond and David Beamish

LONDON

HER MAJESTY'S STATIONERY OFFICE

House of Lords Information Office
Publications series

No. 1.   The Gentleman Usher of The Black Rod
ISBN 0 11 700567 3   Price 60p net

No. 2.   The Lord Chancellor

In preparation

Acts of Parliament

The House of Lords—Its History and Administration

The authors are grateful to members of the staff both of the Lord Chancellor's Department and of the Parliament Office for help in the preparation of this publication.

Front cover:
The Right Honourable the Lord Elwyn-Jones, C.H.,
Lord High Chancellor of Great Britain.

ISBN 0 11 700573 8

The Lord Chancellor

The Lord High Chancellor of Great Britain, as he is formally described in legal documents, is exceptional among public office-holders in the diversity of his responsibilities, which range over all three branches of Government—the Executive, the Legislature and the Judiciary. He is appointed, and may be dismissed, by the Queen on the advice of the Prime Minister, and is a member of the Cabinet with his own Department. He is *ex officio* Speaker of the House of Lords, though strictly he need not be a member of it; in practice he is nowadays always made a peer—if he is not one already—as soon as possible after his appointment, but he officiates as Speaker immediately. Finally, he is head of the Judiciary, and from time to time functions as a judge. The Lord Chancellor's historic and wide-ranging responsibilities are reflected in his being, after the Royal Family, second in precedence in this country, coming after the Archbishop of Canterbury but before the Archbishop of York and the Prime Minister. This booklet gives a brief account of the history of the Lord Chancellor's office and of its present-day duties. A number of sources from which more detailed information on various aspects of the office of Lord Chancellor may be obtained are listed in the Bibliography.

I

The Lord Chancellor in the Middle Ages

From at least the time of the Norman Conquest the King of England had his own secretary who was known as the royal 'chancellor'. This name was derived from the title of the usher in the law courts of the Roman Empire who habitually sat behind the lattice screens of the court. The screens were known in latin as *cancelli*, and the usher was said to be seated *ad cancellos* and was called *cancellarius*. Subsequently, in the Eastern Roman Empire, the *cancellarius* rose in grade from being an usher to serving as a secretary or notary, and it was in this sense that the word was adopted by the Normans. The *cancellarius* or Chancellor was the King's secretary.

The main work of the Norman Chancellor was to supervise the preparation and sending out of the King's letters. These he sealed with the King's seal, the 'Great Seal', of which he therefore became the keeper. The Great Seal seems to have come into existence before the formal office of 'chancellor' developed, since the earliest known seal is that of Edward the Confessor, the last Saxon king but one. The Chancellor was for long invariably in holy orders, was considered 'the most dignified of the royal chaplains', and was often promoted to a bishopric. His office ante-dates the development of Parliament—for the first Chancellor is recorded in 1068, two centuries before Simon de Montfort's Parliament of 1265, which is considered to be the earliest full Parliament.

The Chancellor of 1068, Herfast, was unkindly described by William of Malmesbury as 'of scant intellect and moderate learning', but by the twelfth century men of the distinction of Thomas Becket served as Chancellor (1154–62), and among his mediaeval successors were two who, like Becket, became canonised saints (Thomas de Cantilupe (1264–5) and Thomas More (1529–32)), together with lawyers and administrators of the quality of Archbishop Hubert Walter (1199–1205), Robert Burnel (1274–92) and William of Wykeham (1367–71, 1389–91). Not all Chancellors were clergy; Sir John Lexington, Steward of the Household, was the first lay Chancellor in 1247; the last ecclesiastical Chancellor (or more accurately in this instance, Lord Keeper of the Great Seal) was Bishop Williams of Lincoln, for the years 1621–5. It should be added that the often repeated statement that there has been a woman Lord Chancellor may refer to the occasion in 1253 when Henry III on leaving the realm for Gascony left as Regent his Queen, Eleanor. Some royal letters were then issued under her warrant, but this was given as regent and not as Chancellor—the Chancellor (the Bishop of Ely) continuing to serve.

The office of Chancellor grew up within the royal Chapel, but as the Chancellor's work and status increased, he and his staff (that is, 'Chancery'), separated off from the Chapel and by the early years of Henry III ceased to be an integral part of the Court. By 1245 the Chancery staff had an official residence of its own in the area in which Chancery Lane is situated today. Thus the Chancellor and his staff ceased to follow the King and his chaplains round and acquired a separate status and dignity.

A second office of 'Keeper of the Great Seal', which was a distinctly subordinate one, had already emerged, during the twelfth century (at first as 'Vice-chancellor' or 'Sealbearer'). Such a 'Keeper' was sometimes appointed as well as a Chancellor, though often instead of a Chancellor. It has been suggested that the latter arrangement 'was partly financial economy, but still more to assert the crown's complete control of the great seal', but the practice has now fallen into disuse. The last Lord Keeper was Sir Robert Henley (later Lord Henley), who was Keeper from 1757 until 1761, when he was promoted to be Chancellor. It should be added that

2

there have been occasional periods (for instance from 1689–93, in 1708, 1710, 1756, 1770, 1790 and 1835) when no appointments were made either as Chancellor or as Lord Keeper and the Great Seal was put 'in commission', that is under the control of a named group of individuals. No instance of this practice has occurred since 1835.

Nowadays it is generally recognised that an outstanding feature—probably *the* outstanding feature—of the Lord Chancellor's office is that he is the head of the Judicial system. His judicial functions developed from his task of sealing and issuing letters. Among these were writs ordering attendance at the hearing of a law suit. He soon became a member of the King's Council and even as early as the twelfth century he was frequently hearing pleas in various counties as a Councillor. His work as a judge then developed further in the fourteenth and fifteenth centuries. By 1340 'Chancery' is mentioned as a 'court of law' and it seems likely that the Chancellor was beginning to take over an appreciable portion of the judicial work previously done by the Council as a whole. The Chancellor as councillor and judge sat in a marble chair, which was fixed to the south wall of Westminster Hall, and in front of which, by 1310, was a great marble bench, 12 feet by 3 feet. Both chair and bench stood on a dais of six steps.

The Chancellor thus presiding in Westminster Hall clearly was one of the great men of the realm, a leading Councillor of the King. One of the reforms demanded by the barons in 1244 was that the Justiciar and the Chancellor should be 'elected by all' (that is, of the barons), and on a few occasions in the thirteenth century Chancellors were so elected, but ever since, the Chancellor has been nominated by the Sovereign. Ralph Neville (1226–44) was the last Chancellor to be appointed for life with one exception. Cardinal Wolsey, unknown to Henry VIII it seems, had the phrase *durante vita sua* (for the duration of his life) inserted into a unique patent of appointment. The delivery of the Great Seal was, as it remains, the normal and outward symbol of the Chancellor's appointment. In the absence of the Chancellor the Master of the Rolls was often appointed to be temporary keeper of the Great Seal (but not to preside in Parliament); and he is still one of the commissioners appointed to have custody of the Great Seal in the absence abroad of the Lord Chancellor.

During the thirteenth century the King had begun to hold additional meetings of his Council, attended not only by magnates and ministers but, perhaps from 1225, by elected knights of the shire; and from 1265, by representatives of the towns. Such an expanded Council meeting in 1236 was being called a 'parliament' and by 1300 the word normally indicated the wider and more representative meetings of the advisers of the King.

At such meetings the Chancellor came to play an important and increasingly dominant part. It is difficult to generalise about three centuries during which parliamentary procedure changed quite considerably; during which there were several dynastic revolutions and a civil war; and for which the records of the sittings of parliaments are not extensive, but a number of specific parliamentary functions for the Chancellor can be shown to have emerged during the middle ages.

The first authentic representation of all the constituent elements of Parliament sitting together—that of the Blackfriars Parliament of 1523—is reproduced opposite. It shows an inner ring or square on which sat Councillors who did not have a place elsewhere: the two chief justices, other judges and non-noble councillors. (The number of judges reflects the judicial nature of much of the work of the earlier mediaeval Parliament.) The clerks knelt behind the fourth woolsack in order to compile their minutes. The Chancellor sits, or according to a later illustration stands, at the right of the King, but his normal seat was probably with the chief justices on the upper woolsack. The present arrangement in the Chamber of the House of Lords of a Chancellor's woolsack above two woolsacks in a block thus represents the original seating of councillors. The Lords sat on the outer benches, and the Commons stood facing them.

In the absence of the Sovereign the Chancellor normally presided over the full meetings of Parliament and over meetings of the Lords, but this was not invariable in the middle ages. In some instances a chief justice or other councillor might do so. Moreover, unless created a Lord Spiritual or Temporal, the Chancellor did not himself belong to the House—Chancellor Thomas More presided, for instance, 'without even a casting vote in [the Lords] proceedings'. The Chancellor, incidentally, even if a ʳord, does not seem to have been described as 'the Lord Chancellor' until 1461; he was simply the Chancellor or 'the King's Chancellor'. On the most solemn occasions, the title now is 'the Lord High Chancellor of Great Britain'.

To outward appearances the Chancellor's primary duty within Parliament in the middle ages was to preside over it or, in modern parlance, to sit as speaker. But the full significance of his Parliamentary work was much greater. He was often the main representative of government, that is of the King, in Parliament, and it would be much truer (if somewhat anachronistic) to think of the mediaeval Chancellor as being the Prime Minister. Indeed, the Chancellor seems almost to have been present throughout sessions. The business of a session opened by his preaching a sermon—which was often on the text 'Deum timete Regem honorificate' ('Fear God, Honour the King'), and he included in this sermon, or in a subsequent speech, the King's aims for the Parliament. Thus Chancellor Stillington in 1468 spoke at length on the necessity of going to war with France and obtaining a subsidy for it, and Chancellor Morton (of 'Morton's fork' fame), in 1488, explained how protection was needed for the home markets against foreign competition.

After the opening of a session the Chancellor then took part in debates. In 1386 the Earl of Suffolk, the Chancellor, entered into a spirited debate

PLATE I   King Henry the Eighth opens Parliament at Blackfriars in 1523. This
herald's drawing, the earliest authentic representation of Parliament, shows the
Lord Chancellor, Wolsey, seated on the King's right (near the two chaplains
bearing crosses). The woolsacks are occupied by judges and the Masters in
Chancery.
From the Wriothesley Garter MS, Royal Library, Windsor Castle, by gracious
permission of Her Majesty the Queen.

with Bishop Arundel, as to whether the King should part with the temporalities he held; and, *per contra* (and unusually), Chancellor Booth in 1473 is noted as having 'never ventured to open his mouth'. During the session the Chancellor would take part in Committee work, sometimes reporting the proceedings of the Committee back to the Lords, and as a councillor and leading member of the Lords the Chancellor would receive general petitions to Parliament (specific or individual petitions went to the Clerk of the Parliament) and assist those members who had been nominated 'Triers of Petitions' in dealing with them.

The Chancellor provided a continuous line of communication between King and Parliament. He would deliver instructions from the King, as when in 1406 he instructed the Lords to be daily present in Parliament at 9 a.m. and not to absent themselves (the Commons were told to come at 8 a.m.). And, when necessary, he might adjourn, prorogue or dissolve Parliament on behalf of the King.

Towards the end of the middle ages a more unusual function can be observed which today would be wholly irregular. The Chancellor, when the House of Commons was showing signs of hostility, might visit the House to urge on it the royal will. Thus in 1514 Chancellor Warham led a deputation of peers to the Commons to induce them to grant more money. On a still

PLATE 2 Cardinal Wolsey (facing right in Cardinal's robes) demands a subsidy for King Henry the Eighth from Sir Thomas More, Speaker of the House of Commons. The incident is described opposite. The original painting, by Vivian Forbes (1891–1937), is one of a series of paintings decorating the walls of St. Stephen's Hall in the Palace of Westminster.

more famous occasion, in 1523, Chancellor Wolsey entered the Commons to confront Speaker Thomas More, who subsequently described how Wolsey was attended 'with all his pomp, with his maces, his pillars, his crosses, his pole-axes, his hat and Great Seal too' (see the illustration on page 6). On this latter occasion Speaker Thomas More excused himself and the House from making any answer to the Chancellor's demand for a subsidy of £800,000 (which the Commons complained was more than the whole current coin of the realm). Thomas More himself subsequently became Chancellor and in 1531 entered the Commons with a group of twelve Lords and delivered to them opinions concerning the King's marriage.

These varied examples of the Chancellor's work in Parliament demonstrate how at least until the fall of Wolsey the Chancellor could be reckoned the leading minister of the Crown. Consequently, to this day, the Lord Chancellor retains precedence over all other ministers of the Crown. The modern history of Parliament shows the Chancellor losing his 'Prime Ministership' but retaining a certain, if limited, type of 'Speakership', in the House and then adding to it new judicial functions (as the leading judicially qualified member of the House) quite separate from those he exercised externally in Chancery.

Before leaving the mediaeval Chancellors, it is worth recording a description of one of the last of them, Chancellor Warham (1504–15), which was written by the distinguished Dutch scholar, Erasmus. Erasmus noted that, although already Archbishop of Canterbury, Warham 'was forced to accept the office of Chancellor, which, among the English, is attended with regal splendour and power. As often as he goes into public, a crown and sceptre [he means purse and mace] are carried before him. He is the eye, the mouth-piece, and the right hand of the Sovereign; and the supreme judge of the whole British empire. For many years, Warham executed the duties of this office so admirably, that you would have supposed he was born with a genius for it, and that he devoted to it the whole of his time and thoughts. But all the while he was so constantly watchful and attentive with respect to religion . . . wasting no portion of his time or his spirits in field sports, or in gaming, or in idle conversation, or in the pleasures of the table, or in any profligate pursuit. . . . He rarely suffered wine to touch his lips; and when he was turned of seventy, his usual beverage was small beer, which he drank very sparingly. . . . The hour generally devoted to supper he was accustomed to fill up with prayers or reading, or with telling witty stories, of which he had a great store, or freely exchanging jests with his friends. . . . So this illustrious man made the day, the shortness of which many allege as a pretext for their idleness, long enough for all the various public and private duties he had to perform'.

2

The Lord Chancellor as Speaker of the House of Lords

The Chancellor's place in Parliament, thoroughly well established by the sixteenth century, was given particular emphasis and distinction by the House of Lords Precedence Act 1539. The Act observed that holders of high office had not been given precise places in the House of Lords, and it decreed that the Lord Chancellor as well as the Lord Treasurer, the Lord President and the Lord Privy Seal, if peers, should sit 'on the left side of the said Parliament Chamber, on the higher part of the form of the same side, above all Dukes, except only such as shall happen to be the King's [relatives]'. The various degrees of nobility were to sit 'after their anciently, as it hath been accustomed'.

When the Sovereign was absent, the upper Woolsack remained the Chancellor's seat as Speaker of the House (see the illustrations on pages 10 and 11). Today's practice by which, when the Chancellor takes part in debate, he steps to 'the left side of the Parliament Chamber' and 'goes to his own place as a peer' represents strict adherence to the Act of 1539 (as does the placing of the Lords Spiritual on the right of the throne). The remaining provisions of the Act for seating the Lords seem to have fallen into disuse by the later seventeenth century.

Although the Chancellor sitting on the Woolsack had clearly come to preside as Speaker of the House of Lords it was not fully established that it was his duty so to preside until the Restoration. Then, on 9th June 1660, it was made a Standing Order of the House 'that it is the duty of the Lord Chauncellor, or the Lord keeper of the great Seale of England ordinarily to attend the Lords house of Parlyament'. The Standing Order, with but slight alterations to its wording, is still in force. The duty has been regarded seriously. To take three random examples: Lord Clarendon in 1661 and 1662 attended 143 out of 199 sittings (39 consecutive sittings were missed owing to illness, and a further 16, broken only by one attendance, may have been missed for the same reason). In 1784 Lord Thurlow missed 12 out of 91 sittings, 11 of the 12 being consecutive, and in 1785 he missed none of the 114 sittings. In 1855 Lord Cranworth missed none of 107 sittings. Nowadays chancellors attend continuously unless they have specific leave of absence, often equalling Lord Cranworth's record.

On 3rd February 1722, Lord Macclesfield, Lord Chancellor, arrived at the House over two hours late, without having arranged for his authorised deputy to attend, because, he explained, he had been waiting upon the King and had been detained longer than expected. This excuse was not accepted by the peers, and some, in order to demonstrate their displeasure, moved that the House should adjourn—but the motion was defeated by 49 votes to 31.

On 23rd August 1831, Lord Brougham and Vaux, Lord Chancellor, sought leave to postpone further consideration of the report of the Bankruptcy Court Bill, since his court work would prevent him from being present on the appointed day—for he was holding evening sittings in order to get through his judicial business. Lord Eldon, a former Lord Chancellor, did not think well of this request and reminded the Lord Chancellor that his paramount duty was to be in his place during the House's sittings.

Despite the strictness of the requirement that the Lord Chancellor should attend the House, the Journals record Commissions appointing Deputy Speakers as early as 1566 (on an *ad hoc* basis). Later, it became the practice to appoint a deputy to be available when necessary. Until 1800 there was generally only one Deputy Speaker at a time, but after that date there was usually more than one (and nowadays there are several).

Until 1882, Deputies appear only to have acted when the Lord Chancellor was unable to do so owing to illness or for some similar reason. In that year the House began to sit earlier than previously for public and private business, and it was recognised that this would make it difficult for the Lord Chancellor who, as will be seen, had other public duties, to be present throughout all sittings of the House. Consequently four Deputy Speakers were appointed (in addition to the Lord Chairman of Committees), and the Standing Order requiring the Lord Chancellor to be present has been followed rather less strictly than before. During a day's sitting he may therefore sometimes not be on the Woolsack, but it is still the practice for the Lord Chancellor to seek leave when he has to be away for the whole of a day.

In the absence of any Deputy Speakers appointed by commission, the Lords appoint their own Speaker for the time being—the Standing Order of 9th June 1660 provides that 'in case the Lord Chaunncelor or Lord Keeper of the great Seale bee absent from the house of Peeres, and that there bee none authoris'd under the great Seale from the King to Supplie that place in the howse of Peeres, the Lords may then chuse their owne Speaker during that Vacancy'. All Deputy Speakers appointed since 1837 have been peers. Before that time judges were often appointed—indeed, until the eighteenth century it was more usual for the Deputy to be a judge (Chief Baron of the Exchequer or Chief Justice of the King's Bench or Common Pleas).

Although the Lord Chancellor is described as Speaker of the House of Lords, he does not have the type of power to control proceedings which the Speaker has in the House of Commons. In general the House nowadays controls its own proceedings. For example, whereas in the Commons the Speaker calls members to speak, in the Lords the House decides whom it will hear if two or more Lords rise to speak at the same time. The only power given to the Lord Chancellor is to call to order Lords speaking in the part of the Chamber behind the Woolsack. The duties of the Lord Chancellor as Speaker are otherwise almost exclusively confined to putting questions to the House. Thus when a motion has been moved he rises to declare that 'The Question is that . . .', giving the terms of the motion. Any debate then takes place. At the conclusion of the debate the Lord Chancellor puts the question again, followed by: 'As many as are of that opinion will say "Content". The contrary "Not-content"', pausing for Lords to call 'Content' and 'Not-content' (in contrast to the House of Commons where the calls are 'Aye' and 'No'). Motions are often agreed to without dissent, but if there are calls of both 'Content' and 'Not-content' then the Lord Chancellor judges which side is more numerous and says 'I think the Contents [or Not-contents] have it'. If his opinion is not challenged he goes on to declare 'The Contents [or Not-contents] have it' and the question is decided accordingly. When it becomes apparent—if necessary after repetitions of the expression of opinion—that neither side is prepared to give way, then the Lord Chancellor calls 'Clear the Bar', thereby calling a division. Within three minutes two tellers must be appointed for each side, or a division cannot take place. Provided that both sides have appointed tellers, the question is put again at the end of three minutes, and if both sides persist on this occasion the Lord Chancellor announces: 'The Contents will go to the right by the Throne; the Not-contents to the left by the Bar'. Lords then pass through the division lobbies on either side of the Chamber,

PLATE 3   The Lord Chancellor, Lord Herschell (standing on the right of the picture) about to put the question after the debate on the Government of Ireland Bill. The Bill was rejected, in the early hours of 9th September 1893, by 419 votes to 41. The original oil painting, by Dickinson and Foster, now hangs in a corridor in the House of Lords.

and their votes are recorded. After six minutes the doors of the Chamber are locked, and once the votes have been counted the Lord Chancellor announces the result: 'There have voted—Content: [*number*], Not-content: [*number*]; and so the Contents [*or* Not-contents] have it'.

An occasional but important function of the Lord Chancellor as Speaker

PLATE 4 Lord Simonds, Lord Chancellor 1951–4, seated on the Woolsack in the House of Lords. The Purse is just visible leaning against the Lord Chancellor's back-rest; the Mace also lies on the Woolsack, out of the picture to the right. The original oil painting, by the 4th Lord Methuen, now hangs in a Committee Room in the House of Lords.

is to preside over the Introduction of new Lords. The Chancellor sits on the Woolsack, wearing court dress, black gown, full-bottomed wig and tricorne hat, and a central feature of the Introduction is that the new Lord, kneeling on his right knee, presents his Writ of Summons and (if a temporal Lord) his Patent to the Chancellor. After the Lord has been placed in his appropriate seat he and his two supporters put on their hats or episcopal caps, sit, rise and bow three times to the Lord Chancellor, resuming their seats after each of the first two bows, uncovering at each bow. The Chancellor returns their salutations and when the new Member in procession leaves the House he shakes hands with the Chancellor.

The Lord Chancellor's own Introduction is still more complex (a full description of it is set out in the *Companion to the Standing Orders* (1976), Appendix B). There being no occupant of the Woolsack, the new Lord Chancellor takes his patent and writ from Garter King of Arms and mounts the steps to the Throne, laying the patent and writ on it for a minute before returning to the Table of the House. Salutations are made not to any individual but to the Cloth of Estate, and the Lord Chancellor for this occasion assumes a seat not on the Woolsack but on the Earls' Bench on the right (opposition) side of the House, his historic place as a member of the House and Great Officer of State (rather than as Speaker) mentioned previously on page 8. Subsequently, he takes the accustomed seat on the upper woolsack in front of the Throne.

As Speaker the Lord Chancellor walks in procession from his room to the Chamber at the beginning of each sitting, preceded by his Mace and his Purse. The Mace is placed behind him on the Woolsack, indicating that the House is sitting, and is not removed until the House rises. When the House adjourns the Lord Chancellor returns to his room in procession, again preceded by his Purse and Mace.

Modern Chancellors as Ministers in Parliament

In the middle ages the Chancellor was a dominant figure in Parliament and, as has been suggested, often the most significant of the Ministers of the Crown. In the modern period, from the sixteenth century onwards, although the Chancellor has increasingly consolidated his position within the House of Lords he has tended to lose some of his political grandeur whilst gaining increasing judicial significance.

This process began with the increased importance attached to the post of King's Secretary as a prominent office, notably after the appointment of Thomas Cromwell as Secretary in 1534. Under Elizabeth I and James I, another office, that of Treasurer, carried still more prestige, with Lord Burghley as Treasurer 1572 to 1598, and the Earl of Salisbury Treasurer 1608–12. Each of these processes had a negative effect on the Chancellor's political power. In the following century the emergence of the authority of Sir Robert Walpole as First Lord of the Treasury (1730–42) saw the beginning of a final shift in power with the consolidation of ministerial leadership in the hands of what we now call the Prime Minister.

Even so, certain appointments were made to the Chancellorship of eminent and powerful ministers in the seventeenth century: notably of the Earl of Clarendon (1660–7) and the Earl of Shaftesbury (1672–3), and, although as it now seems quite erroneously, the definitive ecclesiastical enactments of the Restoration period became known collectively as the 'Clarendon code'.

Moreover, Chancellors for long continued to make speeches at the Opening and Prorogation of Parliament. These speeches usually set out the foreign and home policy of the Crown, and by the time of Elizabeth I were sometimes in the words of the Sovereign herself. On one occasion, however, in 1576 when Elizabeth was present, Lord Keeper Nicholas Bacon, according to Sir John Neale, 'had begun to dilate in rather long-winded fashion' when 'the Queen interrupted and commanded him to cease'. Bacon adroitly wound up his speech with the words: 'Lo! My Lords and masters; her Majesty's pleasure is that I shall forbear any further to exhort you ... men so willingly and lovingly disposed, and had rather hazard a part of the thing granted, than to breed any suspicion ... that she is doubtful of your faithful and diligent dealing'. One of the last of the set speeches by Chancellors was that of Shaftesbury who, on 4th February 1673, after King Charles II himself had spoken, made a speech (according to Lord Campbell, the biographer of the Lord Chancellors) 'which for impudence and effrontery far exceeds any to be found in our parliamentary records', though in fact it merely praised the King's own speech and then gave his own highly individual expression to the royal policy. After this speech in 1673, the only orations in full Parliament by the Chancellor seem to have been on such special occasions as when the King was ill (1810), and these were not independent political statements of the Chancellor's own. It should be added, however, that on occasion, as for example, during the reign of George I and part of that of Queen Victoria, and even today, the Lord Chancellor may himself read the Sovereign's Speech at the Opening of Parliament. This has sometimes been in the Sovereign's presence, but in 1963 it was because the Queen was unable to be present. In addition he always reads the Sovereign's Speech on Prorogation.

Lord Chancellors as Parliamentary Orators

What has been more significant for the political life of the country in the modern period than Lord Chancellors' ceremonial speeches has been their day-to-day participation in the work of the House of Lords, normally in support of the group of ministers to which they belonged. The Prime Minister, however, did not always bring the Lord Chancellor into close consultation; on some occasions the Chancellor might not have wished to participate in political debate or, at any rate, to support a particular government measure. Thus, Lord Chancellor Henley (1757–66) confined his utterances to judicial matters. Lord Campbell commented that Henley had 'a pretty strong suspicion in his own mind that he was appointed because he was likely to be quiet in the Cabinet, and he did not seek to interfere. Formal meetings of it were occasionally called which he attended, but he was as little consulted by Pitt about the raising of Highland regiments, or the conduct of the war, as the Six Clerks or the Masters in Chancery'.[1]

Lord Chancellor Thurlow (1778–92) intervened frequently in debate but was of doubtful help to his colleagues. During the latter part of his tenure he was even deprived of his duties as a spokesman for the Government in the Lords: Mr. Pitt, it has been recorded, declared that 'he was very unhappy lest some important measure, on which depended his reputation and his stability, might be defeated, after being carried triumphantly through the House of Commons'. Certainly, Thurlow, in an earlier administration, had spoken against a Bill when he had been expected to move its second reading. Thurlow's manner, according to Campbell, made him initially very unpopular as Speaker of the House of Lords, and he was even taunted with his mean birth. Thurlow replied so powerfully that 'from this time every Peer shrunk from the risk of any encounter with Thurlow, and he ruled the House with a rod of iron—saying and doing what he pleased, and treating his colleagues with very little more courtesy than his opponents'. He was described in the *Rolliad* as, 'The rugged Thurlow who with silent scowl, In surly mood, at friend and foe will growl'.

Lord Camden (Chancellor 1766–70), having had his advice concerning both the Wilkes case and the dispute with America scornfully rejected, thereafter preserved 'an impenetrable silence in Parliament' unless as Speaker he had to put the question and declare the majority. At the other extreme was Lord Chancellor Brougham and Vaux (1830–4) who appears in the *Guinness Book of Records* as having made the longest recorded continuous speeches in both Houses, as a member of the Commons for 6 hours on 7th February 1828, and then, in the Lords, also for 6 hours, on 7th October 1831. The latter speech concerning the Reform Bill concluded with a peroration in the form of a prayer uttered by Brougham on his knees (the editor of *The Complete Peerage* referring to the Chancellor's elaborate peerage title commented that it was commonly said he was '*Vox et preterea nihil*', 'Voice and otherwise nothing').

---

[1] Campbell, who published the first edition of his *Lives of the Lord Chancellors* in 1845 (see Bibliography below, page 39), subsequently himself became Lord Chancellor (1859–61). His contemporary, Lord Lyndhurst, who had served three times as Chancellor between 1827 and 1846, commented that Campbell's *Lives* had 'added another terror to death'. The more recent comment of L. M. Brown and I. R. Christie is that the *Lives*, 'though full of plagiarisms and misrepresentation, contain material not to be found elsewhere' (*Bibliography of British History 1789–1851* (1977), page 88).

Most of the Victorian Chancellors took an active part in debate, contributing in particular to the debates on legal matters, as for example Lord Westbury (1861–5) in pursuing the case for a revision and codification of statute law (1863); Lord Hatherley (1868–72) in supporting Selborne's Judicature Act (1872); and Lord Selborne (1872–4, 1880–5) not only in the passage of his Judicature Act which completely reorganised the higher Courts, but also in a long series of important statutes initiated by Gladstone's Conveyancing Act and the Married Women's Property Act. Lord Chancellor Cairns (1868, 1874–80) had helped Selborne to pass the Judicature Act, and the final settlement of the jurisdiction of the Lords under the Appellate Jurisdiction Act 1876 was his work.

This tradition of active participation in debate was continued in the following reigns. Of more recent Chancellors, one of the most effective as a speaker in debates was Lord Loreburn (1905–12) who as a Liberal was placed in the difficult position of presiding over a predominantly Conservative House during the Parliament Bill debates of 1911. But as has been observed, 'he quickly established a remarkable ascendancy over one of the most difficult audiences in the world'; his 'rugged, plain-spoken Scottish common sense' appealed to the House, and his interventions were listened to with appreciation by his political opponents. When he retired in 1912 the Lords presented him with his portrait, which hangs in the hall of Balliol College, Oxford. Of his successors, Lord Birkenhead (1919–22) was also a distinguished and powerful debater, making for instance, on 16th December 1921, a vital speech in defence of the proposed treaty with Ireland which helped to gain a vote in its favour of 166 to 47.

These random examples covering two centuries show that although the Lord Chancellor in the modern period ceased to hold a 'Prime-Ministerial' position in Parliament he could emerge and frequently has emerged as an outstandingly effective supporter of the Government in the House, and, even when he belonged to a party in a minority in the House, a Minister who could gain great respect and influence within Parliament.

3
The Lord Chancellor
as Judge in Chancery

The Lord Chancellor, meanwhile, had had a separate and equally exacting set of duties as a judge. From the early fourteenth century he sat in Westminster Hall in a totally non-Parliamentary capacity as the judge exercising a common law jurisdiction over suits in which Crown or Chancery officials were involved. Subsequently in that century cases were also presented to him which fell outside the common law administered by the three great Courts of King's Bench, Common Pleas and Exchequer (as, for instance, cases concerning alien merchants, maritime or ecclesiastical matters) and in addition he heard many cases in which, for various reasons, the ordinary courts could not act. The law administered in the Chancery became known as 'equity'; it was in many ways popular and its scope grew, from the sixteenth and seventeenth centuries including cases of fraud and accident. More work meant that the Lord Chancellor needed help; the Master of the Rolls by 1700 was sitting as a judge (from whom appeal could go to the Chancellor) and early in the nineteenth century additional judges called Vice-Chancellors were appointed.

The outcome of individual cases heard in accordance with this more informal type of 'equitable' jurisdiction was often uncertain and it was not until the time of Lord Chancellor Eldon (1801–6, 1807–27) that the doctrines of the Court of Chancery were settled and, as Eldon observed, no longer justified 'the reproach that the equity of this court varies like the Chancellor's foot'. Even so, Chancery remained overburdened and dilatory. Gilbert and Sullivan in 'Iolanthe' gave a relatively genial picture of the Lord Chancellor, the very embodiment of the law, exercising control of the young ward in Chancery, Phyllis the shepherdess, but there was a grimmer literary comment from the greatest of Victorian novelists. Charles Dickens described in *Bleak House* 'this High Court of Chancery, most pestilent of hoary sinners' sitting, as it sometimes did, in Lincoln's Inn Hall, surrounded by a London fog no thicker than the fog in which the case of Jarndyce and Jarndyce had been submerged for decades. The dilatory procedure Dickens described in 1852 was in fact reformed in that very year, the Lord Chancellor thereafter sitting not as judge of first instance, but, if he chose, as a member of a Court of Appeal. Finally, in 1873 came the abolition of the Court of Chancery and the establishment of a new High Court in whose work the Lord Chancellor does not normally participate directly. As will be seen below, the Lord Chancellor remains today the head of the Judiciary, exercising a wide variety of functions. But his personal function as a Chancery Judge ceased in 1875 and since then his judicial work has been almost exclusively performed in the House of Lords and in the Judicial Committee of the Privy Council, which may sit in the mornings when the House of Lords itself is not in session.

4
The Lord Chancellor
as Judge in Parliament

Until the nineteenth century the Lord Chancellor was accustomed to move between two courts: that in Chancery and that in Parliament. The origin of his Parliamentary judicial work can be quite precisely dated to the year 1621. In that year judicial powers of the Lords, only fitfully exercised in the distant past, were revived and augmented.

Original petitions from the public began to be received and determined by the House of Lords (although only until 1693); the process of impeachment of offenders by the Commons before the Lords was revived with the case against the monopolist, Mompesson, in 1621; complaints of technical error in the judgments of various courts were received; and above all, appeals were heard against the actual validity of judgments in courts of law, which, by 1700, included Chancery, Exchequer, Exchequer Chamber, and equity courts in Ireland. After 1707 appeals also came from three Scottish courts— and came in very large numbers during the eighteenth century. This development from 1621 to 1707 meant an immense increase in the daily business of the House of Lords and until at least 1718 the Lords present generally took an active part in hearing the cases, with the Lord Chancellor (or Keeper) presiding. Judgment was given after a division taken in the same way as for legislative business. Where technical points of law were concerned the House might summon judges from the courts at Westminster Hall to give their advice but this was not done in the majority of cases.

The Lord Chancellor is normally recorded as having been present in the House on days when appeals and writs of error were considered, but his was only one vote, as, for example, when in 1713 on Roper v. Hewet *et al.* the appeal was reversed by 53 to 22. Later, during the course of the eighteenth century, the House was to become, like Chancery, a law court under the practical control of the Chancellor, but this development only came during the course of the eighteenth century (the last important general division in the House on judicial business was in 1806, although as late as 1834 a case started without a single Lord 'learned in the law' being present).

Appeals in the later eighteenth century were in practice heard by the Chancellor, with only sufficient fellow peers to make the necessary quorum of three. At some periods there were available to assist him a number of judges, such as Lord Mansfield, who happened to be peers, but there were never more than six of these and occasionally no more than one or two. (They acquired the informal title of 'Law Lords', although the general use of the term only became habitual in the later nineteenth century). However, the Lord Chancellor did not gain continuous expert assistance until the Victorian period. In Eldon's day (1801-6, 1807-27) it was even said that 'appeals in the House of Lords were nothing more than appeals from the Lord Chancellor in one place [i.e. Chancery] to the Lord Chancellor in another place'.

In one capacity, however, the Lord Chancellor had extensive support in his Parliamentary judicial capacity. This was on the occasions when he was chosen to preside over 'the Court of the Lord High Steward'. The court was not usually convened for times when Parliament was sitting, and was used by the Crown (mainly in the seventeenth century) to try peers and conduct State trials. It consisted of a jury of selected peers until 1695 after when the whole body of peers normally participated. The last peer to be tried by the House of Lords, presided over by the Lord Chancellor as Lord High Steward, was a peer accused of manslaughter in 1935. Such trials were abolished in 1948 by the Criminal Justice Act. Perhaps their most dramatic moment (apart from the actual verdict) had been when the Lord High Steward's white wand signifying the court's jurisdiction was broken in two by the Clerk of the Parliaments at the end of the trial.

Judicial sittings of the House in the eighteenth century began at two in the afternoon, and sittings for public business at five o'clock. At the opening of the nineteenth century, the increasing amount of work led to the sitting of the House for judicial business at 10 a.m. (altered to 10.30 a.m. in about 1853). In 1867 came the first formal moves to bring forward the hour at which the House sat for other business. A Select Committee was appointed but recommended no change (by seven votes to six). The matter was raised again in 1878, in 1879, and in 1882, when it was finally agreed to bring the time for non-judicial business, i.e. for bills and debates, forward to 4.15 p.m. Merely providing time for hearing appeals, however, was only part of the problem. More serious was the need to get even a quorum of three (including the Lord Chancellor) to hear the cases. By 1811 there was a queue of 196 appeals and 42 writs of error waiting for consideration and this led to the order that the House was to sit from 10 a.m. to 4 p.m. each day of the week except Saturdays and Sundays. The Lords balloted to provide a quorum to assist the Chancellor for this purpose and Chancellor Eldon commented on how many peers who were 'figuring daily in Hyde Park and the Green Park, could not without fatal consequences, bear three or four hours' confinement [in the Lords]—unless it were confinement for five or six hours at White's or Boodle's at night'.

The eventual outcome of the heavy burden on the Victorian Chancellors in dealing with hundreds of appeals in a year was firstly the creation of Sir James Parke, a member of the Judicial Committee of the Privy Council, as a peer (abortively as a life peer in January 1856, and effectively as a hereditary peer, Lord Wensleydale, in July 1856); and ultimately the Appellate Jurisdiction Act of 1876, which enabled the Sovereign to create four Lords of Appeal in Ordinary, who were to be salaried full-time judges. Originally a Lord of Appeal in Ordinary was able to sit in the House of Lords only so long as he retained his office, but in 1887 this limitation was removed.

The Lord Chancellor up to 1945 still participated for much of the day in the Lords' judicial work. Dr. R. F. V. Heuston has noted that after 1885 the normal day of a Lord Chancellor involved him in presiding over appeals from 10.30 a.m. to 3.45 p.m. or 4 p.m., with half an hour's break for lunch. He then had a quarter of an hour break and returned at 4.15 p.m. for the despatch of legislative business, which occupied him until 7.30 or 8 p.m., 'after which there might be an official dinner as well as the Cabinet papers of the day to be read. Cabinet meetings (usually on Wednesday, but in a crisis more frequently) had also to be fitted in, as well as a mass of administrative business'.

Some earlier sittings of the House had taken place in war-time, and after 1945 the present custom by which the House normally begins its sittings at 2.30 p.m. and not at 4.15 was introduced as a regular procedure. Since 1948 Appellate Committees have been appointed in order to hear causes and report back to the House. Such Committees often sit when the House itself is also sitting. Thus the Lord Chancellor is faced with a choice between acting as Speaker of the House and sitting in the Appellate Committee. In practice, when the House is sitting for non-judicial matters most Lord Chancellors have taken the former choice, but if appeals are heard when the House is not otherwise sitting, the Lord Chancellor may preside over the hearings. On balance, there have therefore necessarily been very few legal judgments by Lord Jowitt (1945–51) and his successors by comparison with earlier practice.

5
The Lord Chancellor
as Administrator

From the moment when the Chancellor began to write and seal the King's letters in the eleventh century administrative responsibilities began to accrue. He needed a staff to help in the preparation of the letters and in enrolling from 1199 'office copies' on Chancery rolls such as the Close Rolls (on which letters 'close' or sealed up were copied) and the Patent Rolls (or letters open, in latin *patentes*). His judicial work in the court of Chancery likewise involved the appointment of officials, and the carrying out of the decisions of the court. Thus a complex group of administrative officials became attached to the Chancellor.

The extensive administrative work of the Lord Chancellor has been, of course, almost entirely within a broadly judicial sphere and he himself has usually been a professional lawyer. The appointment of Sir Christopher Hatton as Lord Chancellor by Queen Elizabeth I in 1587 was probably unique, certainly so in the modern period, in that his previous appointments had not been judicial but had been in the Royal Household—his sobriquet of 'the dancing Chancellor' gives a fair indication of the character of his professional expertise. In the normal course of events since his day, however, Lord Chancellors have not only been qualified in the law but have served as Law Officers of the Crown, that is as Attorney-General or Solicitor-General. This was common practice in the eighteenth and nineteenth centuries, and the tradition is represented today by the present Lord Chancellor, Lord Elwyn-Jones (1974–) who served as Attorney-General from 1964–70. From time to time, however, Lord Chancellors have been appointed who, after initial legal experience, have not served as Law Officers but have held other ministerial posts under the Crown. The previous Lord Chancellor, Lord Hailsham of Saint Marylebone (1970–4), had been Minister of Science and Technology 1959–64 and had also been Leader of the House of Lords from 1960–3. In a single instance, that of Viscount Haldane (1924), the Lord Chancellor served at the same time also as Leader of the House (when in fact there were no other peers in the House of Lords of the party that had come to power). Lord Simonds (1951–4) was a Lord of Appeal in Ordinary at the time of his appointment as Lord Chancellor, and had never held Ministerial office. The same was true of Lord Gardiner (1964–70), who was a distinguished Queen's Counsel in practice at the Bar. Throughout this century Lord Chancellors, whether or not they have previously been Law Officers of the Crown, have always had notable legal experience. This is obviously vital not only on account of their participation in the hearing of causes but also in view of the detailed and elaborate management of legal affairs which, especially within the last decade, has become a primary duty of the Lord Chancellor.

The Great Seal

Before describing the work of the Lord Chancellor's staff attention should be paid to what has been both the principal means of conducting the business and the symbol of the Chancellor's office: the Great Seal itself.

This originated in the middle ages when documents were usually authenticated, i.e. officially authorised, not by a signature, but by a seal made of wax. In the Norman period one of the Chancellor's main functions was to prepare and therefore to seal royal letters. He used a seal later known as the 'Great Seal', which, although varying in size, colour and material over the

PLATE 5   The Great Seal of William I shows, on the obverse (left), the King on horseback, and, on the reverse, the King enthroned. The inscription around the circumference of the obverse reads HOC NORMANNORUM WILLELMUM NOSCE PATRONUM (Know this to be William leader of the Normans) and that around the reverse reads SI HOC ANGLIS REGEM SIGNO FATEARIS EUNDEM (Thus thou acknowledge by this seal the same to be King for the English people).
British Library, Cottonian charters, xxxiv. 3.

centuries, is today recognisably the same sort of seal as that used in the eleventh century (a Great Seal of William I is illustrated above). The term 'Great Seal' came to be used for the matrix itself. This consists of two moulded silver plates which are engraved with appropriate designs and between which wax or a similar substance is pressed in order to produce each individual seal. The Sovereign in person delivers the matrix of the Great Seal into the custody of the Lord Chancellor, and he continues in office until he relinquishes the Seal to the Sovereign. So vital has the Great Seal been for the authentication of documents of the highest importance, and therefore for the maintenance of government, that counterfeiting the Seal was declared high treason by the statute 25 Edward III st. 5, and James II, on fleeing the country in 1688, hoped to make government impossible by throwing the Great Seal into the Thames.

When a new matrix for the Great Seal is brought into use it is laid on the table at a meeting of the Privy Council and when approved is touched by the Sovereign who directs the Lord Chancellor to take custody of it. In the past the old Seal was then broken into several pieces, but in recent times it is the custom for the Sovereign to deface (or to 'damask') the old Seal using for the purpose a special hammer, the head of which is indented. One half of the matrix or both may be presented by the Sovereign to the Lord Chancellor. Usually only one seal is made during a reign unless as in the case of Queen Victoria the reign is a long one. The matrices have been made

PLATE 6   The reverse of the second Great Seal of Elizabeth I shows her riding on horseback, carrying an orb and sceptre, with a rose, fleur-de-lis and Irish harp adorning the background. The inscription around the circumference reads: ELIZABETH DEI GRACIA ANGLIE FRANCIE ET HIBERNIE REGINA FIDEI DEFENSOR (Elizabeth by the Grace of God Queen of England France and Ireland Defender of the Faith). The seal was engraved in 1586 by Nicholas Hilliard, the first English painter of miniatures, and is perhaps the outstanding design in the long sequence of Great Seals.
Public Record Office, SC 13/N3.

of gold, often of silver, now of an alloy principally constituted of silver. The weight of the whole matrix is 18 lb., of which 267 ounces are silver, the Seal having a diameter of 6 inches.

The Great Seal was always affixed in a Chancery Office, or even in the Court of Chancery. Today sealing takes place at the House of Lords in the office of the Clerk of the Crown in Chancery, who since 1885 has also held the office of Permanent Secretary to the Lord Chancellor.

It has been normal for one half of the matrix to show the Sovereign on horseback and the other the Sovereign enthroned (a fine reverse from the reign of Queen Elizabeth I is shown opposite). Until *c.* 1920 the material used for making impressions from the matrix was always wax, but this is a relatively fragile material (as archivists can testify—at least half a typical series of Borough Charters will lack complete seals). Now, therefore, granules of cellulose acetate plastic are used. They are softened in an oven; the matrix itself is also heated. Then the granules are placed in the matrix with the hanging cord of the document laid centrally in the matrix (see the illustration on page 25).

The two halves of the matrix are locked in a steel collar and with the aid of a pump pressure is brought down upon the seal held within the collar. After the matrix and granules have cooled the seal is gently tapped out of the matrix. Colours used for Great Seals have varied: nowadays dark green is used for peerage patents: scarlet red is used for most other patents as, for example for the Royal Assent to the election of a bishop or for a Supreme Court Judge's patent of appointment.

The Great Seal was frequently appended to a very large number of documents prepared on parchment. Over the last century its use has diminished as a result of Rules made under the Crown Office Act 1877 providing that royal proclamations, commissions for Royal Assent, Writs of Summons to Parliaments, commissions of the Peace and many other documents, which had hitherto been handwritten on parchment with the wax seal appended to them, might henceforth be authenticated by the use of a new wafer (single-sided) Great Seal which could be impressed upon documents prepared on paper. This reform proved most successful and at the present time many documents are issued in this manner. The impression currently in use is that of the obverse side of the Great Seal, i.e. the Queen depicted on horseback, and measures three inches in diameter.

The Great Seal at present in use, obverse and reverse, was designed by Mr. Gilbert Ledward, R.A., and approved by the Queen at a meeting of the Privy Council on 1st August 1953. The Seal had been engraved at the Royal Mint.

The device for the obverse is a portrait of the Queen on horseback, wearing the uniform of Colonel-in-Chief, Grenadier Guards, the whole being placed on a plinth of which the upper part appears on the seal. Below the horse is the Crowned Cypher. The legend is in Latin and is the royal title, to be translated as: 'Elizabeth II by the grace of God of Great Britain and Northern Ireland and of Her other realms and territories Queen, Head of the Commonwealth, Defender of the Faith'.

The reverse shows the Queen enthroned and robed, holding in her right hand the sceptre and in her left the orb, her feet resting upon a footstool. On either side of the throne are shields of the Royal Arms. Below the footstool is the legend 'Dieu et mon droit'; and part of the motto 'Honi soit qui mal y pense' appears on the chair behind the Queen's shoulders.

Chancery Administration in the Sixteenth and Seventeenth Centuries

As the Chancellor's work evolved from the purely secretarial several main departments developed. The financial department which had existed from the thirteenth century received the fees or fines paid in and was known as the Hanaper—the same word as the modern hamper (or basket-container). The far larger legal department was staffed by an elaborate hierarchy. 'Masters in Chancery' were the authorities in matters of court practice and procedure and later served as judges in less important cases[1]; the 'Six Clerks' with assistants received and filed legal documents in equity cases; 'Cursitors' made out writs returnable in King's Bench and elsewhere; and 'Registrars' acted as minuting clerks in the court. For day-to-day administration the Chancellor was continuously attended by the Clerk of the Crown who had the special charge of preparing documents for the Great Seal, including writs for summoning peers to Parliament and for electing Members for the Commons, though the preliminary drafting of such documents was a main duty of the 'Clerk of the Petty Bag', the 'Clerk of the Presentations', the 'Clerk of the Dispensations and Faculties', or the 'Clerk of the Letters Patent'.

Some of these offices became sinecures; some were abolished in the early nineteenth century. Then, under the Judicature Act 1873, the separate Court of Chancery was abolished and the present High Court of Justice was established. One of its divisions is still known as the 'Chancery Division' and the Lord Chancellor is the senior judge in the Division. A completely new administrative structure was set up for the High Court and for the Court of Appeal, and only a small group of ancient Chancery offices survive today—among them, those of Clerk of the Crown, Deputy Clerk of the Crown, and Clerk of the Chamber. Within the House of Lords the Clerk of the Parliaments is also in a direct line of succession from office holders in the Chancery of the middle ages.

The Modern Lord Chancellor's Department

At the time of the passing of the 1873 Act the Lord Chancellor had been assisted by a private secretary, his 'Principal Secretary', and by other secretaries with particular duties. These officials were not permanent, but were personal to the Lord Chancellor of the day. Since 1885, however, the Lord Chancellor's Department and the Crown Office have been combined and the officials of the Lord Chancellor's Department have in practice been permanent.

Sooner or later all the matters to be described in this section may come to the Permanent Secretary for decision or for submission to the Lord

---

[1] Masters in Chancery also attended on the House of Lords until the abolition of their office under the Court of Chancery Act 1852. They carried messages and bills from the Lords to the Commons. They were not summoned by writ and were not legal assistants of the House, although they sat with the assistants upon the woolsacks (see the illustration on page 5).

PLATE 7   The Great Seal of the Realm is moulded using a Victorian cast-iron press, shown in this photograph. The process is described on page 23. Formerly the press was operated by a handle placed over the spindle, but it is now operated hydraulically. A Great Seal which has just been moulded is visible in the photograph, with the parchment document to which it is attached wrapped in brown paper to protect it.

Photograph reproduced by courtesy of Courtaulds Limited.

Chancellor. Within Parliament, the Permanent Secretary in his capacity as Clerk of the Crown attends the Commons, standing below the Bar to deliver a Return Book of Members elected at the beginning of each new Parliament; he joins the Clerk of the Parliaments, the Clerk Assistant and the Reading Clerk in the Chamber of the House of Lords for State Openings; and when the Royal Assent is pronounced by Commission the Clerk of the Crown reads out the titles of the bills to be enacted, to which the Clerk of the Parliaments declares severally the Royal Assent.

PLATE 8 Lord Elwyn-Jones, the Lord Chancellor, as Speaker of the House of Lords, presents to Her Majesty the Queen the text of the speech made by him in presenting an address of congratulation from the House of Lords on the twenty-fifth anniversary of her accession. The ceremony took place in Westminster Hall on 4th May 1977.

The Department over which the Permanent Secretary presides is housed partly in offices at the House of Lords, partly elsewhere in London and partly around the country. Its functions are wide ranging, and are not confined to judicial and Parliamentary matters. The Lord Chancellor is always a senior Cabinet Minister and as such is involved in meetings of the Cabinet and those of an increasing number of Cabinet committees. These he attends (and sometimes presides over) not as a legal adviser, but as minister, and in an average week three or four mornings may be occupied by Cabinet work of this type. In addition there are quite frequent foreign visits to be made as official representative of the Government.

The main bulk of the Lord Chancellor's work, however, is concerned with the administration of justice. His Department is not fully a 'Ministry of Justice', since certain aspects of the administration of justice are the responsibility of the Prime Minister, of the Home Secretary, of the Attorney-General, and of the Treasury respectively, but the vast majority of administrative functions in the judicial field are those of the Lord Chancellor.

Perhaps the principal feature of the Lord Chancellor's administrative work is the making of a very large number of appointments. Some relate to the setting up of tribunals, but most are specifically judicial. High Court Judges are appointed by the Crown by Letters Patent, and by long established usage these appointments are made on the recommendation of the Lord Chancellor. The most senior judges are appointed on the recommendation of the Prime Minister, but in practice the Lord Chancellor is always consulted. Circuit Judges and Recorders are appointed by the Crown, but it is specifically provided by statute that such appointments are made on the recommendation of the Lord Chancellor. Since the reign of Edward III the appointment of Justices of the Peace has been the responsibility of the Lord Chancellor. There are now some 24,100 justices and to assist him in their selection he appoints nearly 240 local Advisory Committees. The Lord Chancellor also appoints many court officials, such as Masters and County Court Registrars. Many tribunals of a specifically judicial character are also appointed by the Lord Chancellor, as for example Agricultural Land Tribunals, Industrial Tribunals, Medical Appeal Tribunals and National Insurance Tribunals. It is to the Lord Chancellor that barristers wishing to become Queen's Counsel—to 'take silk'—apply, and he annually recommends to the Sovereign a number of new Queen's Counsel.

At the beginning of each legal year, in October, a service is held in Westminster Abbey, attended by the various ranks of the judiciary, by Queen's Counsel, by junior barristers, and, in recent years, also by distinguished guests invited from abroad, including members of the European Court. After the service the Lord Chancellor traditionally entertains those present at a 'breakfast' held in the Royal Gallery of the Houses of Parliament. (The procession returning to the House from the Abbey is illustrated on page 28).

The same afternoon the Lord Chancellor goes to the Law Courts in the Strand and presides in the court of the Master of the Rolls. Queen's Counsel, led by the Attorney-General and the Solicitor-General, are in their places. The ceremony opens with the Lord Chancellor addressing each by name asking them 'Mr. X, Do you move?', that is, 'have you a motion to raise?'. Each stands, bows and sits down, thus silently indicating a negative, and the ceremony proceeds.

At another annual ceremony, usually taking place in October, the Lord Chancellor receives the newly elected Lord Mayor of London at the House of Lords. In accordance with the Mayoralty Charter of May 1215 the Lord

PLATE 9 The Clerk of the Crown in Chancery and Permanent Secretary to the Lord Chancellor's Department, the Lord Chancellor's Private Secretary, the Lord Chancellor's Pursebearer, and the then Lord Chancellor (Lord Hailsham of Saint Marylebone) lead the procession of judges and lawyers from Westminster Abbey to the House of Lords, after the service traditionally held in the Abbey at the beginning of the legal year in October. Those present at the service are subsequently entertained at the Lord Chancellor's Breakfast, held in the Royal Gallery of the Palace of Westminster (see page 27).

Chancellor signifies the Sovereign's approval of the election and loving cups containing spiced wine are exchanged. Subsequently the Lord Chancellor is entertained at a banquet in the Mansion House.

The daily work of the Lord Chancellor and his staff, occasionally varied by historic ceremonies of this character, is administrative of a normal civil service type, though relating almost entirely to judicial matters. The administration of the Supreme Court (comprising the Court of Appeal, the High Court and the Crown Courts) and the county courts is the responsibility of the Lord Chancellor. England and Wales are divided into six circuits, and a circuit administrator, an official of the Lord Chancellor's Department, is in charge of the administration of the courts in each circuit. He is responsible to the Lord Chancellor. Below him are court administrators, each in charge of a group of courts. The officers and staff administering the courts are appointed by the Lord Chancellor, with the concurrence of the Minister for the Civil Service as to numbers and salaries.

The Lord Chancellor is responsible for a number of bodies which are concerned with legal matters, though their functions are not judicial. Six of these are discussed briefly here.

The Law Commission, together with a Scottish Law Commission, was established by the Law Commissions Act 1965 'for the purpose of promoting the reform of the law'. Its originator was the Lord Chancellor of the day, Lord Gardiner (1964–70), whose tenure of office was particularly distinguished by his zeal for law reform. It comprises a Chairman and four other Commissioners appointed by the Lord Chancellor. It works closely with the Lord Chancellor, making an annual report to him, obtaining his approval for programmes proposed to be undertaken, and preparing at his request programmes of consolidation and statute law revision. The kinds of law reform envisaged by the 1965 Act include codification, the elimination of anomalies, the repeal of obsolete and unnecessary enactments, the reduction of the number of separate enactments 'and generally the simplification and modernisation of the law'.

The Official Solicitor is appointed by the Lord Chancellor. He has been known by that title since 1875, having previously been known as the Solicitor to the Suitors' Fund and then as the Solicitor to the High Court of Chancery. His varied duties include among others applying to the Court on behalf of persons committed for contempt, acting for a poor person when applying for bail, acting as guardian ad litem to persons under disability, and generally acting where the Court considers that the assistance of a solicitor is needed. His department is an office of the Supreme Court.

The Lord Chancellor has for long had duties in connection with lunatics and he now presides over *the Court of Protection.* Historically his function appears to flow from the role of the Crown as protector of those unable to help themselves. Formerly every lunatic had a right to write to the Lord Chancellor, and in 1918 a Royal Commission reported that 'very many lunatics exercise this right—some of them many times a day', though the Mental Health Act of 1959 has led to a gradual reduction in the number of such letters. His duties are now defined by the 1959 Act. The management of the property of persons under disability is undertaken by the Court of Protection, an office of the Supreme Court, whose officers are appointed by the Lord Chancellor. The Lord Chancellor also appoints Medical and Legal Visitors of Patients, known as the Lord Chancellor's Visitors. It is their function to investigate matters relating to the capacity of any patient to manage and administer his property and affairs.

The Public Trustee Act 1906 created the office of *the Public Trustee.* This officer is appointed by the Lord Chancellor and operates under rules made by the Lord Chancellor. His function is to act as trustee of wills and settlements, pension funds, disaster funds, etc. and as executor or administrator of estates. Fees are charged, so that the office is self-supporting.

The Land Registry Act 1862 made general the concept of registration of land (originally introduced for Yorkshire and Middlesex). This was initially a voluntary arrangement, though later enactments have made it compulsory in certain areas. The Act also set up a *Land Registry* to administer the scheme, and from the outset the Land Registry was subject in various ways to the control of the Lord Chancellor. Certain appointments in the Land Registry are made by him, and he makes (with the advice of others) rules and orders relating to the registration of land.

The Public Records Act 1958 placed *the Public Record Office* under the direction of the Lord Chancellor. This office has the custody of the records of the Courts and of Government Departments including such famous documents as Domesday Book and the Gunpowder Plot papers, and is one of the world's great storehouses of historical material. For long it was under the direction of the Master of the Rolls. But this meant that there was no Government Minister responsible to Parliament for the office. So, from 1959, the Lord Chancellor took over responsibility, with the Master of the Rolls retaining custody of the records of the Chancery of England and acting as Chairman of an Advisory Council on Public Records appointed to advise the Lord Chancellor. The Lord Chancellor appoints a Keeper of the Public Records and presents to Parliament an annual report on the work of the Public Record Office.

The Ecclesiastical and Visitatorial Duties of the Lord Chancellor

A non-legal aspect of the Lord Chancellor's work of long standing is his extensive ecclesiastical patronage—he is patron of over 600 benefices, as well as of certain other benefices which lapse to the Crown. This is an onerous duty involving the interviewing of those considered to be suitable candidates and the holding of appropriate consultations locally. His ecclesiastical functions also include a duty to serve as one of the Church Commissioners and he is Visitor to several corporate bodies such as St. George's Chapel, Windsor, and may receive the Sovereign's instructions to act on Her behalf in the affairs of corporations of which the Sovereign is Visitor.

Keeper of the Royal Conscience

Finally reference must be made—and at this point it is perhaps particularly appropriate—to what has been described as the Lord Chancellor's duty to act as 'Keeper of the Royal Conscience'. This has sometimes been taken to mean that the Chancellor, in the time when he was usually a bishop, was the King's confessor. In fact, however, the King's confessors were not Lord Chancellors. The first Lord Chancellor to have described himself as Keeper of the Royal Conscience appears to have been Lord Chancellor Hatton in 1587. According to him it is 'the holy conscience of the Queen, for matter of equity, that is in some sort committed to the Chancellor'. In other words, the Lord Chancellor's duty to act as Keeper of the Royal Conscience relates to his equitable jurisdiction in the Court of Chancery. It has sometimes been said that the Lord Chancellor's position as Keeper of the Royal Conscience is a bar to the holding of the office by a Roman Catholic. In fact, however, legal doubts about the eligibility of Roman Catholics to hold the office were founded on nineteenth century statutes and the Lord Chancellor (Tenure of Office and Discharge of Ecclesiastical Functions) Act 1974 makes clear that Roman Catholics may hold the office.

Conclusion

Over some nine centuries the office of a single royal scribe has developed into a large and complex department of State. Today the Lord Chancellor has under his direction some ten thousand civil servants and the annual expenditure of the department is of the order of £70 million. The overall balance of work has shifted from parliamentary to administrative and is reflected in the present allocation of only £2,500 of the £20,000 annual salary[1] to his work as Speaker. The Lord Chancellor's ancient duties in Parliament and the High Court, however, remain substantial and it is hard to imagine the Upper Chamber not being presided over by a Lord Chancellor. A. P. Herbert once described an incumbent of the office (Lord Jowitt) as a one man band, 'a human orchestra complete Who played the cymbals with his feet …. And never ceased to strike a multitude of drums and things'. The Lord Chancellor is a dramatic exception to what Montesquieu had regarded as the significant feature of the British Constitution and what is today an important feature of the American constitution, a separation of powers between Legislature, Executive and Judicature, for the Lord Chancellor has played for most of the nine hundred years of his office an important and often a leading part in all three.

[1] This salary has developed from an ancient and intricate series of allowances, one of which was £96 a year in lieu of 12 tuns of Gascon wine. From 1700, salaries were regularly paid to the Lord Chancellor. Eventually the Lord Chancellor's Salary Act 1832 eliminated allowances and specified a salary of £10,000 a year (see a Memorandum by J. C. Sainty on 'The Remuneration of the Lord Chancellor', in the House of Lords Record Office).

Appendices

(A) *The Maces*

Maces were originally weapons of offence—metallic clubs with flanged or spiked heads having some type of simple hand-grip. In the later middle ages they also became a symbol of certain types of authority, notably royal or civic. The club end became smaller and rounder while the handgrip end tended to be enlarged and decorated with heraldic devices. Such maces would then be carried 'upside-down', i.e. with the arms at the top and the club end at the bottom.

Certain servants or 'serjeants' in the Royal Household carried maces in the later middle ages and when in 1415 the House of Commons first obtained the services of a royal Serjeant-at-Arms he would have come to the House with his mace. In 1543 the Commons claimed that their order to arrest should be executed 'by their Serjeant without writ, only by shew of his mace, which was his Warrant'.

The date of the origin of the office of Serjeant-at-Arms attending the Lord Chancellor cannot be established with precision. Wolsey is credited with having a silver mace borne before him and it is very likely that Chancellors were then having maces carried before them, but no Serjeants specifically attached to the Lord Chancellor are recorded before 1550. From then on a Serjeant-at-Arms attended the Chancellor at all times, i.e. he appeared at sittings of the House, in the Court of Chancery, and elsewhere.

An early express mention of the Lord Chancellor's mace is in 1677. On the 7th November the mace was stolen from the then Lord Chancellor, Lord Finch (later Earl of Nottingham): 'About one in the morning the Lord Chancellor Finch his mace was stole out of his house in Queen Street. The Seal laid under his pillow, so the thief missed it. The famous thief that did it was Thomas Sadler, soon after taken and hanged for it at Tyburn'.

For long there have been two maces at the House of Lords, and it has been suggested (but apparently without positive evidence) that the theft in 1677 was the reason for having a 'reserve' available. However, in 1827 the two maces were described as 'The House of Lords Mace' and 'The Court of Chancery Mace', the latter being the Lord Chancellor's mace proper. So it could—though this is pure conjecture—be that the reason for having two is that one is strictly the mace of the Speaker of the House of Lords while the other is strictly the mace of the Lord Chancellor, in whatever capacity. Another reason which has been given for there being two maces is that in the first half of the eighteenth century deputies who were not Serjeants-at-Arms sometimes acted for the Lord Chancellor's Serjeants-at-Arms. Since they would not have maces formally issued to them, a second mace

PLATE 10   Lord Hailsham of Saint Marylebone, Lord Chancellor 1970–4, in the robes worn on ceremonial occasions, with the Purse and Mace.

may have been provided for their use when the Lord Chancellor's was not available. Nowadays only one of the maces is normally used—the other is used only occasionally, for instance when the Lord Chancellor attends the Lord Mayor's Banquet (at which time the first mace is normally in use in the House).

The mace is used by the Lord Chancellor as a symbol of Royal authority, both in the House of Lords and elsewhere when he appears officially. However, the mace is not used when the Sovereign is present. Thus in 1965, at the ceremony in Westminster Hall to celebrate the seven hundredth anniversary of Simon de Montfort's Parliament, although the Lord Chancellor was accompanied by his mace, it was covered on the Queen's arrival (as was Mr. Speaker's mace). This practice was again observed in Westminster Hall in 1977 when the Queen was presented with Addresses by both Houses on the occasion of the Silver Jubilee of her reign (see the illustration on page 26).

The mace now in use is believed to date from the time of Charles II. It is of silver gilt, 5 ft. 1 in. in length, and weighs nearly 22 pounds. It may not have been in continuous use in the House of Lords since it was made, but was certainly being used there frequently in the seventeenth century and probably in the eighteenth as well. It has been used continuously in the House of Lords at least since 1827, and is probably the mace described in 1827 as the 'House of Lords Mace'. It is shown in the illustrations on pages 28 and 33.

The second mace dates from 1695 when it was made for the Lord Chancellor's serjeant. It has been held in the House of Lords ever since. It, like the first mace, is of silver gilt, is 5 ft. 1 in. long, and now weighs 23 pounds. It is supposed to have increased in weight, having undergone many repairs and alterations since it was first made.

(B) *The Lord Chancellor's Purse*
The use of a special purse to hold the Great Seal (i.e. the matrix of the Seal) can be traced back as far as the end of the thirteenth century. An Exchequer Roll of the year 1298 has a drawing of such a purse in the margin of a memorandum relating to the Great Seal. At the beginning of the fourteenth century a red purse was in use. In 1353 six shillings were spent on a purse for the Great Seal. In the fifteenth century a bag of white leather seems to have been used. But in 1515 Wolsey became Chancellor, and it was said that in order to gratify his love of show 'the simple bag in which the Great Seal was deposited, which for centuries before had been composed of linen or of leather, and which, when delivered to him, was "a bag of white leather", was transformed to a magnificent purse, something like that which is now carried before the Chancellor, being described as "a bag or purse of crimson velvet, ornamented with the arms and emblems of England".'

PLATE 11 The Lord Chancellor's Purse formerly contained the Matrix of the Great Seal of the Realm. It is now used to hold the text of the Gracious Speech made by the Queen at the State Opening of Parliament; the Speech is handed to the Queen by the Lord Chancellor. The empty Purse is carried before the Lord Chancellor in procession.

At about this time it became the custom for a new purse to be procured annually. The purse of the later sixteenth century is shown in a portrait of Lord Keeper Nicholas Bacon of 1579; the purse was gathered at the top. James I is said to have devised some additions of gold embroidery. It is recorded that seventy pounds was paid for a new purse in 1801. In 1872 the practice of supplying a purse once a year (doubtless justified originally when 17 pounds of Seal was carried around in it) came in for criticism in the House of Commons, and it was decided that the purse should be renewed less frequently after the death of a very old lady who had a vested interest in the supply of them. She died in 1873 and thereafter purses (costing £65 each) were expected to last for three years.

When a new purse is provided, the old purse is the perquisite of the Chancellor. According to one authority, 'the wives of two Chancellors who held office for several years apiece are stated to have had so many of them that they caused them to be made up into curtains'. Old purses are also said to have been used to adorn chairs and a firescreen.

It is not recorded when the purse ceased actually to hold the Great Seal. But there is a legend that an eighteenth century Chancellor dropped the purse, which did at that time hold the Great Seal, and so heavy was it that it broke a bone in his foot. Today the purse is normally empty, but is used to hold the Queen's Speech at the State Opening of Parliament.

Modern purses are shown in the illustrations on the cover and on pages 33 and 35.

(C) *The Lord Chancellor's Robes*

The mediaeval Chancellors, being usually churchmen, would have worn either their ecclesiastical robes or their episcopal Parliamentary robes. The present Lord Chancellor's robes are post-Reformation and their design seems to date from the late sixteenth century (see the illustration on the cover).

Today, when acting as Speaker of the House of Lords, the Lord Chancellor wears a black cloth court suit, and over it a black silk gown with train. On his head he wears a full-bottomed wig. The wig was apparently adopted at the same time as the Judges' (in the later seventeenth century) when wigs were fashionable, and continued to be worn by judges after they went out of fashion. Before that, Lord Chancellors simply wore a layman's hat of the period. The tricorne hat, now only worn on ceremonial occasions, had become fixed as the hat of the Chancellor by the early eighteenth century.

The Lord Chancellor's State robe is of black damask embroidered with gold lace. It is not exclusive to the Lord Chancellor, being also the official robe of the Speaker of the House of Commons and of the Chancellor of the Exchequer. Judges of the Court of Appeal and Chancellors of Universities wear a similar robe on State occasions. The Lord Chancellor seems to have first worn this kind of robe in the late sixteenth century. During the sixteenth century the custom of decorating gowns with 'guards' of material grew up. Among wealthy officers gold lace was used—a portrait of the Speaker of the House of Commons in 1554 shows such a robe, similar to that worn today.

The first Chancellor to appear in a portrait dressed in such a robe was Sir Christopher Hatton (1587–91); Hatton, to whom reference has already been made, is said to have had flamboyant tastes (one account describes him as 'a gay young cavalier never called to the bar, and chiefly famed for his handsome person, his taste in dress, and his skill in dancing'), and this doubtless explains his adoption of this kind of robe. From the beginning of the seventeenth century a robe of this type appears to have become the official robe of the Chancellor. It was retained, after the general Tudor fashion died out, during the seventeenth century. It had previously been worn by Privy Councillors and other men of dignity, which has led to the suggestion that it is a Privy Councillor's robe (this would explain why it is now worn by Judges of the Court of Appeal). But, in fact, it probably originated simply as a lay costume for wealthy and eminent men. The Lord Chancellor's robe has remained unchanged since the seventeenth century, apart from a lengthening in the form of a short train.

The State robe is worn in the House of Lords at the Opening of Parliament. The Lord Chancellor has yet a third form of ceremonial dress. This is his cloak or ordinary Peer's robe, velvet and ermine, which he wears in the House (together with full-bottomed wig and tricorne hat) for Royal Commissions.

(D) *The Lord Chancellor's Residence*

Nowadays the visitor standing on the River Terrace sees towers at the northern end of the Houses of Parliament which contain the residence of Mr. Speaker and those at the southern end containing the residence of the Lord Chancellor. The Lord Chancellor's residence, however, unlike the Speaker's, is a relatively recent innovation. The Lord Chancellor always had a working room or office in the Palace but no bedroom or residence, and Barry, the architect of the Houses of Parliament, merely provided office accommodation on the west front for the Lord Chancellor and his immediate staff. The southern towers by the river were built by Barry in the 1850s to contain a residence for Black Rod; then, for a time, the Clerk of the Parliaments occupied them, and it was only in 1917 that the proposal was mooted that the Lord Chancellor should live within the Palace. Lord Chancellor Cave in fact resided in the Palace during the 1920s. In 1944 the proposition was revived at a Joint Select Committee on Accommodation in the Palace of Westminster, and as a result the residence now in use was provided on the first floor of the southern tower overlooking the river and the Victoria Tower gardens.

(E) *The Lord Chancellors of Scotland and Ireland*

This booklet has concentrated on the history of the Lord Chancellor of England before 1707, and of the Lord Chancellor of Great Britain since that date, when the kingdoms of England and Scotland were united. The first Lord Chancellor of Great Britain was Lord Cowper, who had previously been Lord Keeper of England, and it is true to say that in general the Lord Chancellor of Great Britain inherited the traditions of the English Lord Chancellor. However, there had also been a Lord Chancellor of Scotland since at least the early twelfth century. The last Lord Chancellor of Scotland, the Earl of Seafield, was appointed in 1705, and in fact retained the office after the Union until his death in 1730, except for a time when he held the office of Lord Chief Baron of the Exchequer in Scotland. Until 1707 Scotland had its own Parliament, consisting of a single chamber, over which the Lord Chancellor normally presided, though he was not regarded as *ex officio* president until after the Restoration. A statute of 1661 declared him to be president 'in all meetings of his Majesty's Parliament or other public Judicatories of this Kingdom'. His other duties were similar to those of the English Lord Chancellor, and included the custody of the Great Seal of Scotland.

The earliest record of a Lord Chancellor of Ireland dates from 1189. The duties of the Irish Lord Chancellor came to be very similar to those of the English Lord Chancellor, and he acted as Speaker of the Irish House of Lords. In 1800 the Irish Parliament was abolished, but there continued to be an Irish Lord Chancellor who was a judge and head of the Judiciary in Ireland, Keeper of the Great Seal of Ireland, and a member of the Government. The last appointment of a Lord Chancellor of Ireland was that of Sir John Ross in 1921. He ceased to be Lord Chancellor when the office was abolished by statute in December 1922.

Select Bibliography

Although no major works on the history or functions of the Office of Lord Chancellor have been written there is an immense mass of biographical references and much incidental comment in legal text books. The following items were used in the preparation of the present booklet.

A list of Lord Chancellors is printed in the *Handbook of British Chronology*, ed. F. M. Powicke and E. B. Fryde, 2nd ed. (Royal Historical Society, 1961), pp. 80–9. Lists of Clerks and Deputy Clerks of the Crown in Chancery are provided by J. C. Sainty in *Officers of the House of Lords, 1485 to 1971* (House of Lords Record Office Memorandum No. 45, 1971).

A list of Lord Chancellors of Scotland is given in the *Handbook of British Chronology*, and a list of Lord Chancellors of Ireland up to 1890 is given in the *Book of Dignities* by Joseph Haydn (London, 1890). A manuscript list of Irish Lord Chancellors from 1890 to 1922 compiled by J. C. Sainty is available in the House of Lords Record Office.

Biographies appear in Lord Campbell, *The Lives of the Lord Chancellors and Keepers of the Great Seal of England* ... [to 1859], 5th edition (London, 1868); J. B. Atlay, *The Victorian Chancellors*, 2 vols. (London, 1906–8); and R. F. V. Heuston, *Lives of the Lord Chancellors, 1885–1940* (Oxford, 1965).

The authoritative works on the Great Seal are A. B. Wyon, *The Great Seals of England* (1887) and H. Maxwell-Lyte, *Historical Notes on the Use of the Great Seal of England* (HMSO, 1926). The records and administration of Chancery are described in *Guide to the Contents of the Public Record Office*, vol. i (HMSO, 1963). The general legal history of Chancery and the Lord Chancellor receives frequent mention in W. S. Holdsworth, *History of English Law*, 17 vols. (1903–72).

Descriptions of the various duties of the Lord Chancellor are to be found in three Presidential addresses to the Holdsworth Club of the University of Birmingham (all given by Lord Chancellors in office):

Viscount Hailsham, *The Duties of a Lord Chancellor*, 1936
Lord Gardiner, *The Trials of a Lord Chancellor*, 1968
Lord Hailsham of Saint Marylebone, *The Problems of a Lord Chancellor*, 1972

A description by a former Permanent Secretary to the Lord Chancellor is Lord Schuster, *The Office of the Lord Chancellor*, in volume 10 of the Cambridge Law Journal, page 175ff. (1949).

An account of the work of the Lord Chancellor's Department is given in the *Report of the Machinery of Government Committee* (Cd. 9230) 1918, chapter x.

Descriptions of ceremonials in the House of Lords in which the Lord Chancellor participates are to be found in the *Companion to the Standing Orders and Guide to the Proceedings of the House of Lords* (HMSO, 1976).

Printed in England by McCorquodale Printers, Ltd., London
and Published by Her Majesty's Stationery Office
HM 7866 Dd 586704 K40 8/77 McC 3339